To my vanilla, my butter pecan, and my chocolate.

−S.L.P.

Giving thanks to God for blessing me with a beautiful wife who inspires me and for putting together such a special group of children for me to photograph.

−M.C.P.

ISBN 0-439-14892-8

Text copyright © 2000 by Sandra L. Pinkney.
Photographs copyright © 2000 by Myles C. Pinkney.
All rights reserved. Published by Scholastic Inc.
SCHOLASTIC and associated logos
are trademarks and/or registered trademarks of Scholastic Inc.

Library of Congress Cataloging-in-Publication Data

Pinkney, Sandra L.
     Shades of black : a celebration of our children / by Sandra L. Pinkney ;
photographed by Myles Pinkney.
        p.   cm.
     "Cartwheel books."
     Summary: Photographs and poetic text celebrate the beauty and diversity of African American children.
     ISBN 0-439-14892-8
     [1. Afro-Americans— Fiction.]   I. Pinkney, Myles C., ill. II. Title.

PZ7.P63348 Sh   2001
[E]—dc21

                 99-086593

12 11 10 9 8 7 6 5 4 3 2   00 01 02 03 04 05

Printed in Mexico   49

First printing, November 2000

SHADES *of* BLACK

A CELEBRATION OF OUR CHILDREN

by Sandra L. Pinkney ✢ Photographs by Myles C. Pinkney

SCHOLASTIC INC.

New York Toronto London Auckland Sydney Mexico City New Delhi Hong Kong

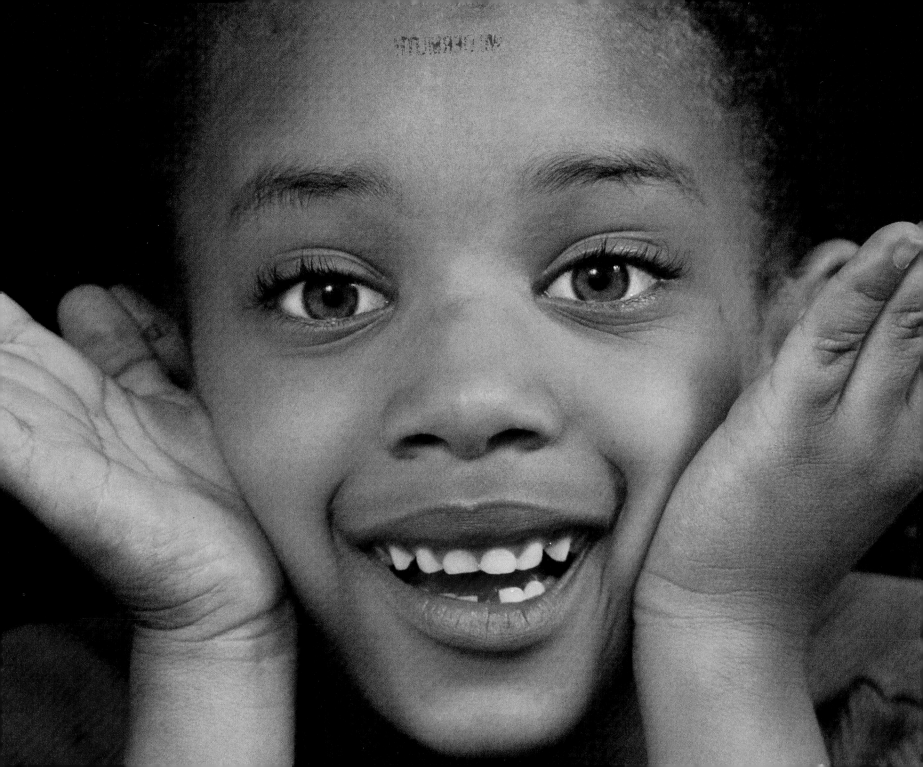

I am Black

I am Unique

I am the **creamy white** frost

in **vanilla** ice cream

and the milky

smooth brown in a chocolate bar

I am the
midnight blue
in a licorice stick

and the
golden brown
in sugar

I am the
velvety orange
in a peach

and the
coppery brown
in a pretzel

I am the
radiant brassy yellow in popcorn

and the **gingery brown**

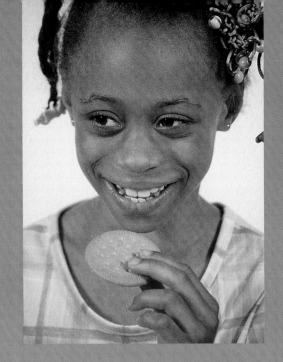

in a **cookie**

I am Black

I am Unique

in a **cotton ball**

My hair is the **soft puffs**

and the **stiff ringlets** in lambs wool

My hair is the **straight** edge

in a **blade of grass**

and the **twisted** corkscrew

in a **rope**

WILDERMUTH

My hair is short

and my hair is long

All of my hair is good

I am **Black**

I am **Unique**

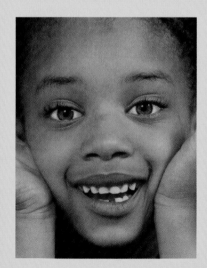

My eyes are

the delicate **streaks of amber**

in a Tiger's-Eye

and the
warm luster of green in a Unakite

My eyes are the brilliant flash of blue in a Lapis

and the shimmering glow of ebony in an Onyx